PULBOROUGH
SCHOOL
LIBRARY
- 6 SEP 1995

FIRST TECHNOLOGY
Energy

Author: **John Williams**
Photography: **Zul Mukhida**

'I want to know what makes things go,' said Zoe looking at me.
'No time for questions now my pet. We're late! Just eat your tea.'
'But Mummy, how do hamsters run, and blue tits learn to fly?
How do caterpillars crawl? I don't like Shepherd's pie!'
'Now Zoe! Come on. Eat it up! Look Michael's eating his.'
'But Mum, I might be best at Games, if I know what it is.'
'Best at Games. Now let me see. Oh Mike! Not on the floor!
The thing you need is energy, that's what your food is for.'
'Energy ... in pie and peas? Now Mummy are you sure?'
'Right that's enough! It's time to go!'
'Oh Mum ... I want some more!'

Wayland

FIRST TECHNOLOGY

Titles in this series

Machines

Tools

Wheels and Cogs

Energy

Toys

Packaging

Series editor: Kathryn Smith
Designer: Loraine Hayes

© Copyright 1993 Wayland (Publishers) Ltd

First published in 1993 by
Wayland (Publishers) Ltd
61 Western Road, Hove
East Sussex BN3 1JD, England

British Library Cataloguing in Publication Data

Williams, John
Energy – (First Technology Series)
I. Title II. Series
333.79

ISBN 0 7502 0714 0

Typeset by DJS Fotoset Ltd, Brighton, East Sussex.
Printed and bound in Turin, Italy, by Canale.

Words printed in **bold** appear in the glossary on page 31.

The publishers would like to thank Gamleys of Hove for the loan of the toys in this book. All the photographs in this book were taken by Zul Mukhida, except for the following: J. Allan Cash 22; Bruce Coleman 12 (Uwe Walz); Eye Ubiquitous 11 (Felix Kerr); Timothy Woodcock 27 (right).
The poem on page 1 is by Catherine Baxter.

WARNING: Children should always be supervised when handling any electrical equipment or machinery.

Energy makes things work and move. Our bodies use energy all the time...

...when we are sleeping

We get our energy from the food we eat.

We eat breakfast, lunch and dinner every day to give us plenty of energy.

When we swallow food it is **digested**. Then our bodies can use it to give us energy.

These children are eating their lunch. Which of these foods will give them the most energy?

10

Plants need energy to grow.
Plants get light energy
straight from the Sun.
The Sun shines on their leaves.

Some animals eat plants. They get their energy from the leaves, seeds or fruit of plants.

Ruskin is eating a fish.

Some animals eat other animals to get their energy.

There are many other kinds of energy.

This lamp needs **electricity** to make it light up. It uses **electrical energy**.

This **calculator** needs sunlight to make it work. It uses light energy.

If you beat a drum, the noise you make is sound energy.

The flame on this candle gives out heat energy and light energy.

Heat energy is easily wasted. This hot water bottle has a thick cover to keep the heat in.

There are two more special kinds of energy.

Something has waiting energy when it is waiting to move.

The child at the top of this slide has waiting energy.

The wound up rubber band on this toy has waiting energy.

What do you think will happen when Katy lets go of the toy?

The answer is on page 32.

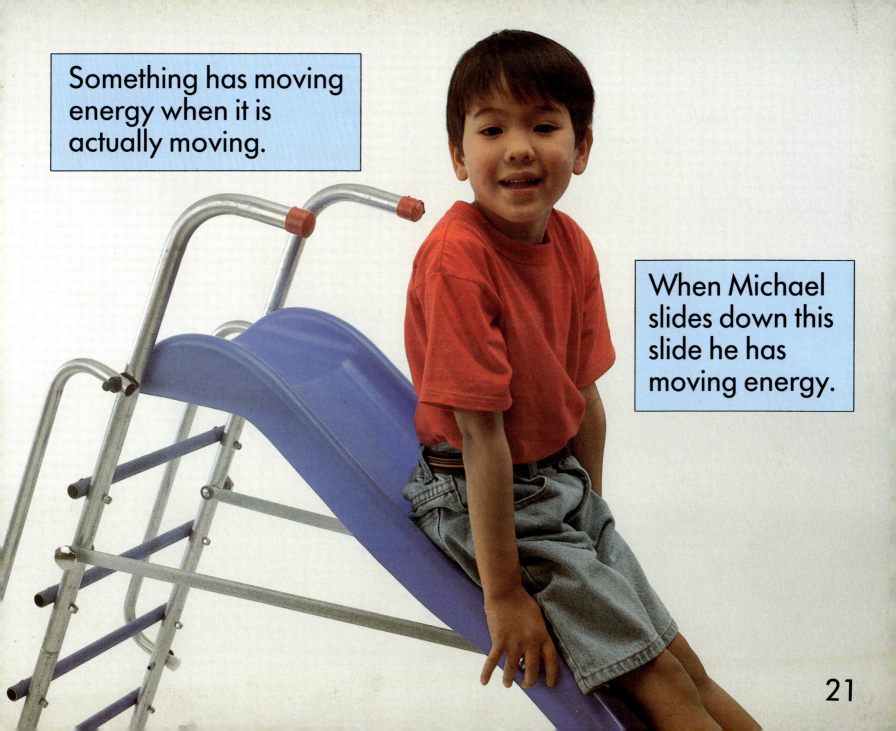

Something has moving energy when it is actually moving.

When Michael slides down this slide he has moving energy.

21

There is moving energy in this machine when it is working. The wheel turns round and round.

What sort of energy does this ball have when Katy throws it into the air?

Michael is waiting to throw this ball. What sort of energy do you think the ball has?

The answers are on page 32.

There are lots of different types of energy being used in these pictures.

Electrical energy

Sound energy

Light energy

Heat energy

How many kinds of energy can you see being used in your school?

These four pictures show four different kinds of energy; sound energy, food energy, waiting energy and moving energy.

Which type of energy is in each picture?
The answers are on page 32.

Using energy – making a simple paddle boat

> You will need a square-shaped plastic bottle, a small piece of soft balsa wood, two pieces of wood (1 cm square and 45 cm long) and some rubber bands.

1. Fix the long pieces of wood to the plastic bottle with rubber bands.

2. Staple a rubber band to the middle of the piece of balsa wood.

3. Put the piece of balsa wood between the two long pieces of wood.

28

4. Wind up the rubber band to make the paddle go round.

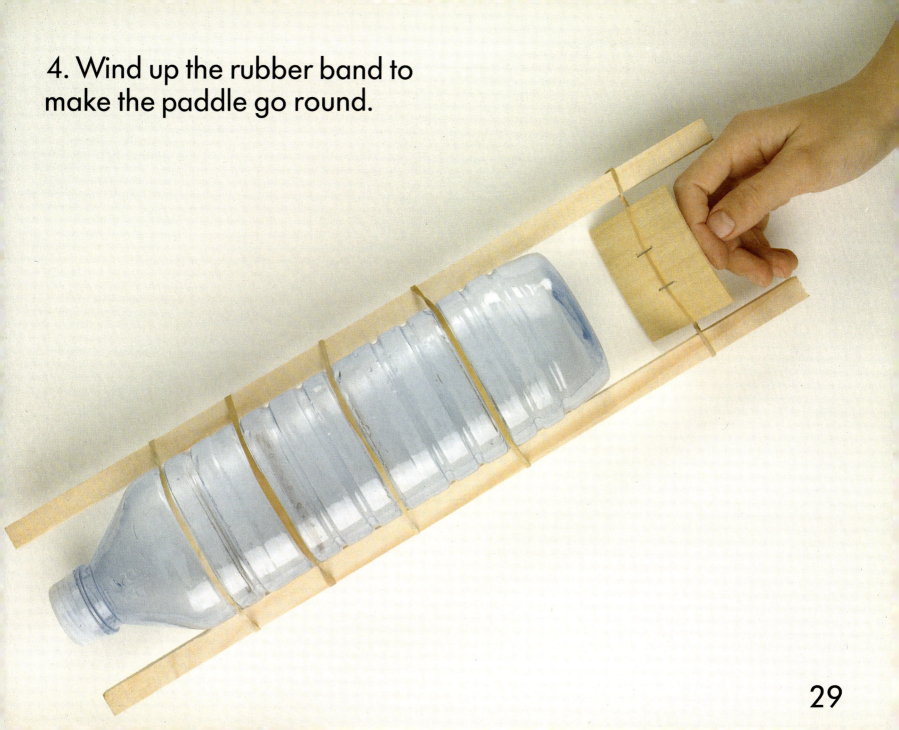

NOTES FOR TEACHERS AND PARENTS

Energy is a very abstract concept, and difficult for young children to understand. However, energy produces motion and makes activity and work possible. It is therefore important for children to be introduced to the concept at an early age. This book enables children to look at various forms of energy within their own experience, and gives them concrete examples of how energy works.

Children of this age will probably have experience of simple food chains. It should be understood that energy moves through food chains, starting with energy from the sun and ending with the chemical energy released when food is digested. The chemical energy released is then converted by the body into other forms of energy, and the energy chain goes on.

In fact, energy is never destroyed, but is simply converted from one form to another.

All energy can be converted from one form to another. The production of electricity is a good example of this. Coal or oil is burnt to produce steam, which drives the turbines that produce the electricity. Electricity may be used for various purposes, all of which involve one form of energy or another.

To keep the language in this book simple, potential energy is described as waiting energy, whilst kinetic energy is described as moving energy. An object has potential energy when it has the potential for motion or activity. Kinetic energy may be defined as the energy associated with movement. Although mechanical energy is not mentioned in the text, parents and teachers should be aware that it is a combination of potential and kinetic energy, which together produce motion and do work.

Potential energy is difficult to understand, because it does not seem to do any work. How, for instance, can a stationary object have energy? If it were allowed to fall on a tin tray, then the resulting sound energy could be used as an alarm clock.

Using energy

The paddle boat activity has been tested on children in both primary and nursery schools. It gives children the opportunity to put their basic knowledge into practice. The potential energy of the wound-up rubber band is converted to kinetic energy as it unwinds, producing the mechanical energy of the rotating paddle.

GLOSSARY

Digested When the food we have eaten is broken down into tiny bits, so that our bodies can use it for jobs.

Calculator A special machine that we use to do sums.

Electrical If something is electrical, it works using electricity.

Electricity Energy that can travel along wires. It is used to give heat and light, and to make many different machines work.

Energy Something which allows work to be done. There are many different kinds of energy.

Machine Something that can help us to do work. Machines can be very simple, like a tin opener, or very large and complicated, like the machines used in factories.

INDEX

animals 12, 13

bodies 4, 7
breakfast 6

digested 7
dinner 6

electrical energy 14, 24
electricity 14

food 6, 7
   bread 9
   cereal 8
   eggs 8
   fish 8, 13
   fruit 8, 12

meat 8
pasta 9
potatoes 9

heat energy 17, 18, 25

light energy 11, 15, 17, 25
lunch 6, 10

moving energy 21, 22

plants 11, 12

sound energy 16, 24, 26

sunlight 15
Sun, the 11

waiting energy 19, 20, 21

Answers to the questions on pages 20, 23, 26 and 27

page 20 The rubber band will unwind, and the toy will fly.
page 23 When Katy throws the ball, it has moving energy. When Michael holds the ball, it has waiting energy.
page 26 Shaking a tambourine makes sound energy. Eating an apple gives food energy (chemical energy).
page 27 The child swinging on a swing uses moving energy. The child waiting to jump has waiting energy

Malcolm Penny

WHALES

Illustrated by
Colin Newman

Language Consultant:
Diana Bentley
University of Reading

PUFFIN BOOKS

Words printed in **bold** are explained in the glossary

Contents

What is a whale? 4
Whales with teeth and
   whales without teeth 6
The biggest whales of all 8
Singing whales 10
Travelling whales 12
Sperm whales 14
Killer whales 16
Pilot whales 18
The smallest whales 20
A whale is born 22
Captive whales 24
Whales and people 26
Can the whales come back? 28

Glossary 30
Books to read 31
Index 32

What is a whale?

Whales are huge animals that look like giant fish, but they are not fish at all! They are mammals.

All mammals have warm blood and they breathe air. They feed on milk from their mother.

Whales have no back legs, and instead of front legs they have **flippers**. Their tails have wide **flukes** at the side to help them swim. Whales keep warm by being covered in a thick layer of fat. This fat is called **blubber**.

Humpback whales

Whales with teeth and whales without teeth

There are two types of whale, some with teeth and some without.

Whales without teeth have **baleen** instead. Baleen is like a row of huge brushes in the whale's mouth. The whale takes a mouthful of water and spits it out through the brushes. The brushes trap the small animals that are in the water. The whale eats these animals for food.

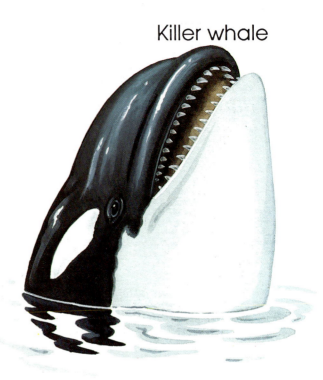

Killer whale

Humpback whale

The small animals which whales eat are called krill. Krill are like shrimps. They swim in the water in enormous **swarms.**

Grey whale

The biggest whales of all

Blue whales are the biggest whales. They are the biggest animals that have ever lived on Earth. A blue whale can grow up to 30 metres long and can weigh more than 135 tonnes. It can be longer than a swimming pool and heavier than three large lorries.

Blue whales have baleen instead of teeth. They feed on krill and small fish. They have to catch many thousands of fish or millions of krill every day.

Singing whales

Humpback whales sing under water. The males growl and whistle so loudly that they can be heard by other whales many kilometres away. In the days before ships had engines, sailors lying in their **bunks** at night used to be able to hear the whales singing.

Humpback whales have baleen, not teeth. They live in warm seas in winter, but in summer they swim nearer the North or South Pole, where there is more food for them in the cold water.

Travelling whales

Grey whales travel very long distances every year. They swim thousands of kilometres, from near the North Pole to the coast of Mexico, to have their babies. People go out in small boats to see the whales. Some grey whales are so **tame** that they let people pat them.

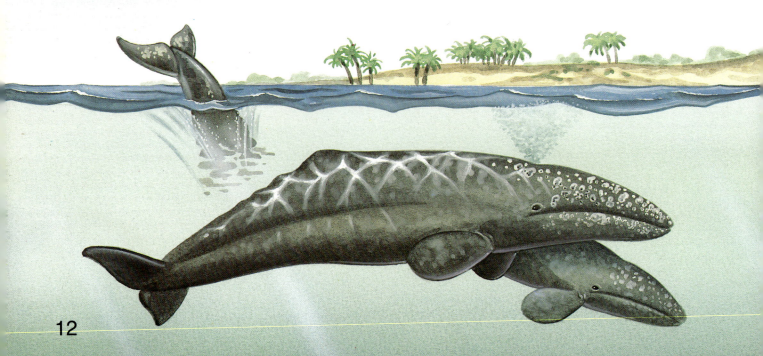

Grey whales feed by scooping up mud from the bottom of shallow water, and then sieving it through their baleen.

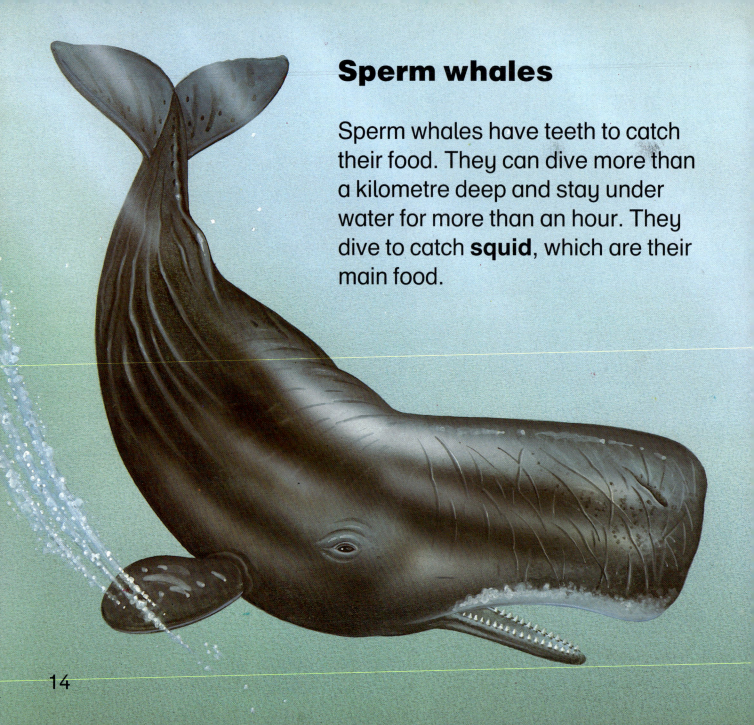

Sperm whales

Sperm whales have teeth to catch their food. They can dive more than a kilometre deep and stay under water for more than an hour. They dive to catch **squid**, which are their main food.

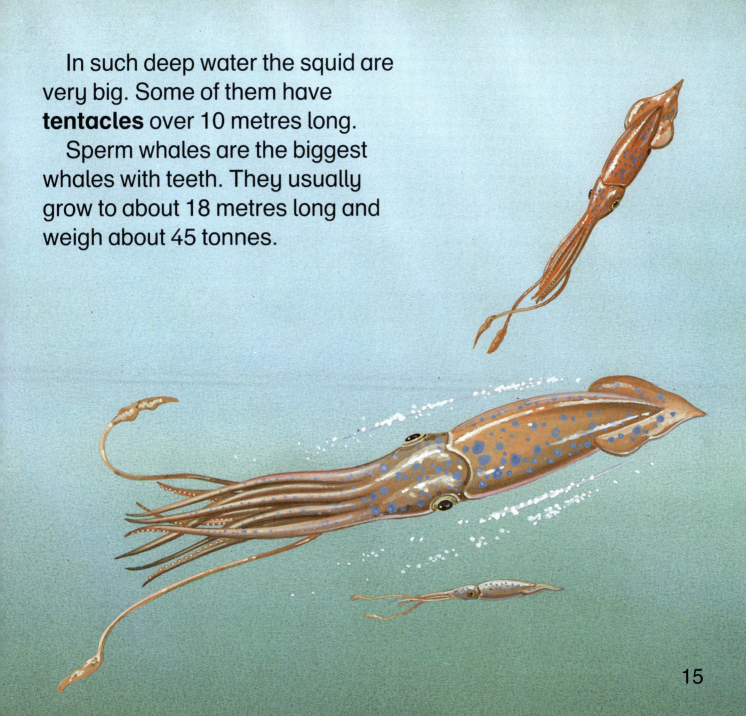

In such deep water the squid are very big. Some of them have **tentacles** over 10 metres long.

Sperm whales are the biggest whales with teeth. They usually grow to about 18 metres long and weigh about 45 tonnes.

Killer whales

People used to think that killer whales were very fierce and dangerous. Now we know that they are quite gentle and intelligent.

Killer whales have teeth. They feed mostly on fish but also eat seals, penguins and porpoises.

Killer whales live in families, called **pods**. The families keep together by making whistling sounds to each other. When they hunt they make buzzing sounds. The sounds bounce off fish in the sea so that the whale can hear where its food is.

Pilot whales

Pilot whales were given their name by fishermen who believed they would show them the way to where the best fish could be caught. They are black and only about 6 metres long, which is small for a whale. Sailors often see pilot whales in the Atlantic Ocean.

Pilot whales are very friendly to people. At one time the American Navy trained them to fetch things from the bottom of the sea.

Pilot whales have teeth. They can dive very deep to find squid to eat.

The smallest whales

The smallest whales are porpoises and dolphins. There are many different types living in different places all over the world.

Dolphins are very playful animals. They often jump out of the water, spinning round or turning cartwheels. They are friendly and easy to tame. Sometimes they are kept in **captivity** so that people can watch them performing tricks.

Dolphins and porpoises can swim very fast. This helps them to catch fish in their sharp teeth.

A whale is born

It is very unusual to see a whale being born because this normally happens out at sea or in a small bay where people do not go. Once, in America, a killer whale mother gave birth to her baby in a big pool where people could watch.

As the baby's head appeared, the mother rolled over and over in the water until the baby popped out. The baby could swim straight away and soon went to the surface of the pool to take its first breath of air. The baby was over 2 metres long.

Captive whales

A pool where whales and dolphins are kept in captivity is called a dolphinarium. The biggest whales to be kept in a dolphinarium are killer whales and pilot whales. Many people think that it is cruel to keep such big animals in a pool.

However, dolphins seem to be quite happy in captivity. They become very tame and people like to watch them. A lot of what we know about whales comes from watching captive dolphins.

Whales and people

Long ago, American Indians hunted whales for food and for their blubber, which they melted to make oil. They went out in **canoes** and would only kill one whale, leaving the others.

Later, whale oil became very valuable. Men came in large ships to kill the whales. Soon they had killed many thousands of them, until there were very few left.

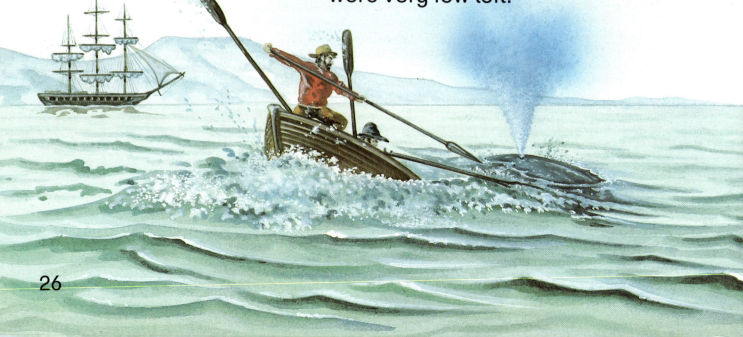

Whaling has almost stopped now. We do not need to hunt whales because we can get oil from other sources. Sadly, people from some countries still kill whales.

Can the whales come back?

Grey whales have recovered from whaling. There are now almost as many of them as there were before whaling started. Other great whales, like blue whales and humpback whales, are still very **rare**.

In the Antarctic, near the South Pole, where whales were once very common, other animals like to eat krill. There are now more penguins and seals because there has been plenty of food for them while so many whales were being killed. Now that the penguins and seals are eating the krill, there might not be enough for the whales.

Can the big whales come back? We shall have to wait and see.

Glossary

Baleen   The row of brushes which a whale without teeth uses to catch its food.

Blubber   The layer of fat which keeps a whale warm.

Bunk   A bed on a ship.

Canoe   A small light boat used by Indians.

Captivity   This means keeping a wild animal in a cage or pool.

Flippers   A whale's front legs, which are shaped like paddles to help it swim.

Flukes   The flaps on the sides of a whale's tail.

Pod   The name for a group of whales.

Rare   Not often seen, very few in number.

Squid   An animal like an octopus, but with ten legs instead of eight.

Swarm   A large crowd of small animals, like ants or bees. Large crowds of krill are called swarms.

Tame   Gentle, not wild.

Tentacles   The rubbery 'arms' of a squid, which it uses when feeding.

Whaling   Hunting for whales, for food or for their blubber.

Books to read

Whales and Dolphins, Lionel Bender (Franklin Watts, 1988)
Whales and Dolphins, Terence Wise (Wayland, 1980)
Whales of the World, Lyall Watson (Hutchinson, 1981)
A Year in the Life of a Whale, John Stidworthy (Macdonald, 1987)

Index

A
America 23
American
 Indians 26
 Navy 19
Antarctic 29
Atlantic
 Ocean 18

B
Baleen 6, 9, 10, 13
Blubber 5, 26
Blue whales 8–9, 28

D
Dolphinarium 24

Dolphins 20–1, 24–5

F
Flippers 5
Flukes 5

G
Grey whales 7, 12–13, 28

H
Humpback whales 4–5, 6, 10, 28

K
Killer whales 6, 16–17, 23, 24

Krill 7, 9, 29

P
Penguins 16, 29
Pilot whales 18–19, 24
Pods 17
Porpoises 16, 20–1

S
Seals 16, 29
Sperm whales 14–15
Squid 14, 15, 19

W
Whaling 26–7, 28